P9-DCD-755

Welcome

Imagine calling this marvelous country estate "home."
From 1839 to 1969 three generations of the du Pont family
did just that.

Jacques and Evelina du Pont Bidermann, their nephew
Henry Algernon du Pont, and his son Henry Francis
du Pont all have left their mark on the estate. Over the
years, they built and expanded a magnificent mansion filled
with priceless antiques; developed the land with working
farms; and created an enormous naturalistic garden among
the rolling hills. They also took great pride in sharing their
treasure with others—entertaining both family and friends
in grand style.

Today, as then, guests remain a vital part of the
Winterthur estate. Since 1951, when the property opened
to the public, visitors from all parts of the world have expe-
rienced the pleasures of our "country place."

We invite you, as well, to become part of the Winterthur
tradition. Read about our unique history, tour our impres-
sive museum of decorative arts, and stroll our lovely garden.
The estate is yours to enjoy!

LESLIE GREENE BOWMAN
Director

Contents

Introduction

Winterthur offers a rare combination of beauty, history, art, and learning. Nestled in the scenic Brandywine Valley of Delaware, Winterthur is the former home of Henry Francis du Pont, a scion of the family whose industrial achievements played a significant role in American history. Immediately upon entering the estate, visitors encounter tangible reminders of its past. Rolling meadows, fresh-water ponds, stone bridges, greenhouses, dairy barns, a vast garden, workers' housing, and an imposing mansion all remind us of the days a century ago when Winterthur figured prominently in the American country estate movement. In the late 1920s the property encompassed more than 2,600 acres and housed some 250 resident workers. It consisted of numerous farms; the finest dairy herd of Holstein-Friesian cattle in America; an expansive, wooded landscape with naturalistic garden; and a family manor house that provided the perfect setting for country-house weekend entertaining.

While developing the family home as a country estate and collecting the finest of American decorative arts, H. F. du Pont was also beginning to envision a wider role for his Winterthur—one that would eventually include opening the mansion and grounds to the public, offering all a glimpse of life in the past: "My idea of Winterthur is that it is a country estate museum, to show Americans of the future what a country place and farm were like." Since 1951, our guests have enjoyed just that experience.

Today Winterthur's 1,000-acre estate offers much for visitors to explore: a world-class museum of decorative arts that celebrates the best in style and craftsmanship; a romantic landscape of incomparable beauty that imparts the peace and great calm of a country place; a naturalistic garden that combines the art of horticulture and landscape design; and a superlative research library that supports Winterthur's graduate programs in early American culture and art conservation.

We invite you to discover our fascinating history...our world set apart.

Genealogy

*Pierre Samuel
du Pont de Nemours*

(1739–1817)
Publisher and economist

*Eleuthère Irénée
du Pont de Nemours*

(1771–1834)
Founder of E. I. du Pont
de Nemours & Co.

Louise Evelina du Pont
(1877–1958)

Henry du Pont
(1812–1889)
Partner, E.I. du Pont de Nemours
& Co., and gentleman farmer

Henry Algernon du Pont
(1838–1926)
U.S. Senator and
gentleman farmer

Pauline Louise du Pont
(b. 1918)

Henry Francis du Pont
(1880–1969)
Gentleman farmer, collector,
and founder of Winterthur Museum
& Country Estate

*Evelina Gabrielle
du Pont Bidermann*
(1796–1863)

Ruth Ellen du Pont
(b. 1922)

The
History

PIERRE SAMUEL
DU PONT
DE NEMOURS

ELEUTHÈRE
IRÉNÉE
DU PONT
DE NEMOURS

The Early Years

COMING TO AMERICA Winterthur's story begins in France in the late 18th century. Pierre Samuel du Pont de Nemours, a French statesman and intellectual, was imprisoned during the French Revolution for his support of a constitutional monarchy. Although sentenced to the guillotine, he survived and left France in 1799 with his family to seek refuge in the new United States of America.

The group that traveled from France—seven adults and six children—landed in Newport, Rhode Island, on New Year's Day, 1800. The family initially planned to establish a business in New York City but abandoned the idea. Desperate to support his wife and three children, Pierre Samuel's younger son, Eleuthère Irénée, drew on his experience as a manufacturer of gunpowder. After obtaining the necessary capital from European investors, he purchased a 95-acre parcel of land, Hagley, on Brandywine Creek near Wilmington, Delaware. It was there in 1802 that he established E. I. du Pont de Nemours & Co. for the production of "Brandywine powder." He also built the first du Pont family home in the Brandywine Valley, called Eleutherian Mills.

THE BIDERMANNS Wars and embargoes alike contributed to the early success of du Pont's powder company, but there were insufficient funds to pay dividends to investors. In a fortunate twist of fate, Jacques Bidermann, one of the largest European investors, sent his son, Jacques Antoine, to Wilmington to review the financial health of the business. Bidermann determined that the venture was financially sound, and he calmed the investors' fears. More important, he and du Pont developed a fast friendship. When Bidermann offered to remain in Delaware and work for the company, du Pont accepted. He was equally enthusiastic several years later when Antoine Bidermann asked for the hand of du Pont's daughter Evelina in marriage.

THE NAME "WINTERTHUR" In 1837, after many years of service, Bidermann retired from the company. He sold his interest in the business and with Evelina and their son, James Irénée, he sailed for France. After only two months abroad, however, the Bidermanns returned to Delaware and took up residence on 450 acres of land they had purchased from the estate of Evelina's father. Antoine wrote to a nephew, "I am more than ever decided to end my days near you…I shall not feel at home except near the Brandywine." Situated among the rolling hills of northern Delaware with a meandering stream known as Clenny Run, the Bidermann property seemed the perfect place to call home. Antoine and Evelina built a 12-room Greek-revival manor house

Eleutherian Mills, ca. 1870

JACQUES
ANTOINE
BIDERMANN

EVELINA
DU PONT
BIDERMANN

The Brandywine Valley in the 1800s

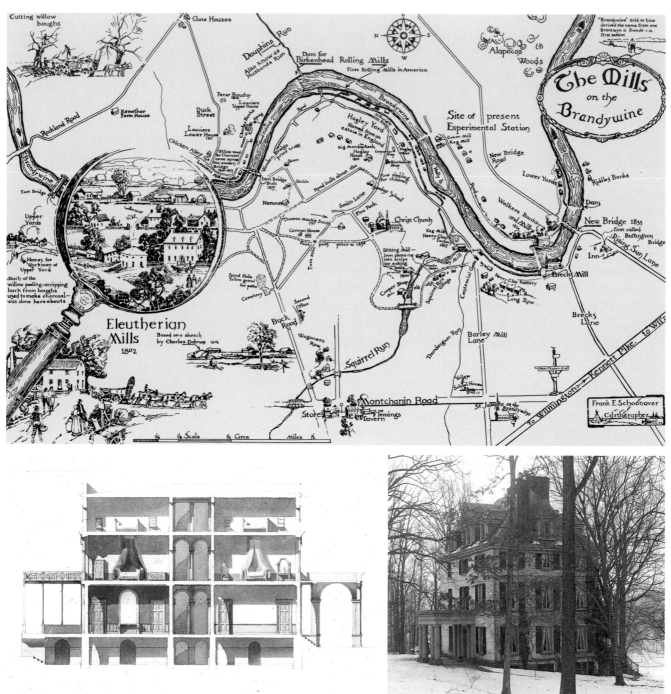

Proposed house design, ca. 1839

The Winterthur house, ca. 1884

HENRY
DU PONT

HENRY
ALGERNON
DU PONT

MARY PAULINE
FOSTER
DU PONT

LOUISE
EVELINA
DU PONT

HENRY
FRANCIS
DU PONT

11

and named the estate after Antoine's ancestral home, Winterthur, Switzerland.

Over the next 25 years, the Bidermanns devoted their energies to developing the country estate with flower, fruit, and vegetable gardens, livestock, and pasture land. When they died in the mid-1860s, their son sold the property to his uncle Henry du Pont, Evelina's brother, writing, "I am sure now that all my father's works will be respected and continued if possible." Although Henry lived at Eleutherian Mills, he made many improvements to the Winterthur property, which contained some 23 buildings in the 1860s. His intent in keeping the land in the family was to provide a home for his eldest son, Henry Algernon.

Henry Algernon: Plans for Expansion

THE COLONEL It seems fitting that Henry Algernon, who was known as the Colonel, would live at Winterthur. He had been a favorite nephew of his Aunt Evelina and Uncle Antoine and spent many happy years on the estate. He was also his father's child: multitalented, autocratic, a superb horseman, and devoted to the family. Henry Algernon followed in his father's footsteps and entered the military, graduating first in his class from West Point in 1861. Commissioned a second lieutenant in the Corps of Engineers, he was rewarded for his bravery in the Civil War—promoted first to major and then to lieutenant colonel for "distinguished service at the Battle of Cedar Creek." Years later he was awarded the Congressional Medal of Honor.

MARRIAGE TO PAULINE FOSTER In 1874 the Colonel married Mary Pauline Foster, a young woman from New York society. The couple set off on a year-long honeymoon trip to Europe, where they were introduced to both the du Pont and Bidermann relatives.

When they returned to the United States, Henry Algernon resigned from the military, and the couple moved to Winterthur in the spring of 1876. Although the younger du Ponts lived at Winterthur, Henry still owned the property, and both father and son involved themselves in renovations to the estate and house. They expanded the road system, made modest changes to the interior of the house, and added a raised roof in 1884. Responding to news of the change, one friend wrote to Pauline, "It must look quite a castle."

Henry Algernon and Pauline loved Winterthur. The garden, the grounds, and the pristine setting all contributed to the allure of their home. And it was at Winterthur that their children Louise and Henry Francis were born, in 1877 and 1880.

MAJOR HOUSE RENOVATIONS In 1889 Henry du Pont died. Soon after, Henry Algernon and Pauline began making plans to remodel on an unrestrained scale. Renovations included an addition that housed many of the accoutrements essential to country estate life: a squash court, a billiard room, a library, a new drawing room, and an imposing marble stairway in the then-fashionable Beaux-Arts style. The facade of the house changed just as dramatically: Francis I-style dormers, a Mediterranean tile roof, and terra-cotta cornices all contributed to a stately appearance. The original Bidermann house was now totally enveloped.

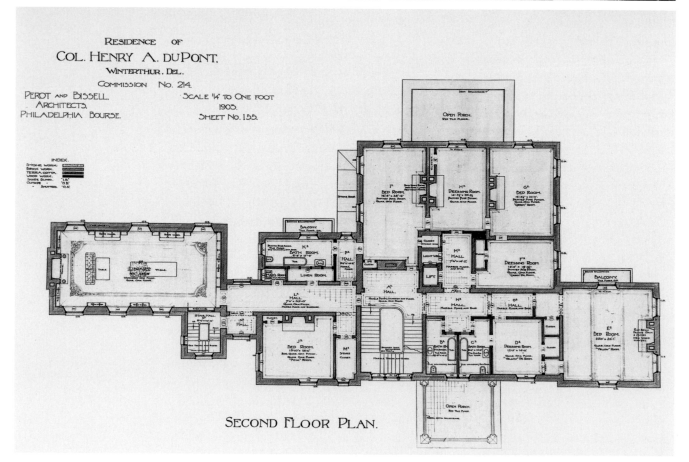

Henry Francis: Developing the Estate and Museum

YOUNG HARRY Henry Francis du Pont shared his parents' love of the land. He spent many hours learning the names of flowers, planting and tending a garden, and arranging bouquets. For Harry, as he was called, his mother and the garden at Winterthur became synonymous with everything that was beautiful. At a young age, Harry began to collect bird eggs, minerals, and plants. Later in life he told an interviewer that he "must have been born with it [the collecting instinct]."

In 1893 Harry was sent to boarding school at Groton, Connecticut. He then continued his studies at Harvard, where, at the beginning of his third year, he wrote of his "sudden resolution" to pursue the study of horticulture: "Flowers, etc. are the only real interests I have." In 1901 he enrolled in Bussey Institute, a Harvard program that focused on the practical aspects of agriculture and horticulture. Energized by this new course of study, he began making plans to attend graduate school.

NEW RESPONSIBILITIES In September of 1902, after a long illness, Pauline Foster du Pont died at her daughter's home in Massachusetts. For Harry it was a devastating blow. From the tragedy of his mother's death, however, came a new direction for the 22-year-old. He spent the better part of his Harvard senior year at Winterthur, helping his father with details of the massive renovations his parents had undertaken. Harry assumed his mother's role in managing the Winterthur house. Overseeing the servants, selecting furnishings for the new wing, and participating in landscaping decisions gave him a new focus. He showed talent, and his father made him manager of the household in 1903. Under the direction of father and son, the estate grew to include its own train station, coach house, and more than 20 greenhouses, potting sheds, and cold frames.

When Henry Algernon was elected to the United States Senate in 1906, he established a residence in Washington, D.C. and put Harry in charge of the household there as well. In further recognition, the elder du Pont appointed his son head of the garden at Winterthur in 1909 and manager of Winterthur Farms in 1914. Henry Francis now oversaw the entire property.

MARRIAGE TO RUTH WALES It was in Washington that H. F. du Pont first became acquainted with Ruth Wales, the niece of Elijah Root, a senator from New York and secretary of state under Theodore Roosevelt. Ruth was

The Train Station

Early greenhouses on the estate

RUTH WALES
DU PONT

PAULINE
LOUISE
DU PONT

RUTH
ELLEN
DU PONT

View to the house, 1909

H. F. du Pont's prizewinning Holstein-Friesians

raised in Hyde Park and was a talented musician. After four years of courtship, the couple became engaged in May 1916 and married two months later. In the next six years, Harry and Ruth were to have two daughters, Pauline Louise and Ruth Ellen. They also established a residence in New York City and later added a summer place in Southampton and a winter retreat in Florida. Winterthur, however, always remained "home."

A TALENT FOR MANAGEMENT: THE FARMS
Following his appointment in 1914 as manager of Winterthur Farms, the younger du Pont reorganized the estate's structure. He created farms that concentrated on one specialty—pigs, turkeys, cattle, sheep, and so on—and also studied and practiced crop rotation. But the majority of du Pont's attention was focused on improving the dairy herd, which produced milk for those living on the estate as well as the residents of nearby Wilmington. He spent hours developing a better strain of Holstein-Friesian cattle, one that would produce milk with a high butterfat content. His father enthusiastically endorsed this goal, writing that it was a "splendid idea...which will do a lot for humanity." The success of du Pont's scientific approach to breeding, registry testing, and record-keeping resulted in an astonishing number of awards and citations. And to house his prizewinning herd, du Pont constructed state-of-the-art barns with reinforced concrete floors for insulation, fireproof doors at the hay chutes, and an elaborate ventilation and temperature-control system.

A TALENT FOR COLLECTING: THE ANTIQUES In 1923 Ruth and Harry traveled to Shelburne, Vermont, to study the cattle-breeding operation of W. Seward Webb at Shelburne Farms, but the most memorable part of the trip occurred in the home of the Webbs' daughter-in-law, Electra Havemeyer Webb, who collected American decorative arts. This was the moment, as H. F. du Pont loved to recount, when he fell in love with American antiques: "I hadn't thought of American furniture at all, I went upstairs [at Electra Webb's] and saw this dresser...this pine dresser and I thought it was charming, quite lovely. It just took my breath away."

On this same trip, the du Ponts visited the summer residence of Henry Davis Sleeper in Gloucester, Massachusetts. Sleeper, an interior decorator, had converted his home into a showcase for American antiques, displaying the objects in rooms made up of paneling, doors, windows, and fireplaces from various early American interiors. Sleeper's ideas further fueled du Pont's interest in Americana. Inspired by both the Webb and Sleeper houses, H. F. du Pont returned to Delaware determined to build his own collection of American decorative arts as well as a house to

Winterthur Farms letterhead

The dairy barn complex, ca. 1928

hold that collection.

CHESTERTOWN HOUSE: THE FIRST PHASE

In 1923 H. F. du Pont purchased a large tract of beachfront property in Southampton, Long Island, where his family had summered for several years, and began building Chestertown House, his first "American" home. Following Sleeper's example, du Pont purchased paneling from early American homes (many from the small riverport town of Chestertown, Maryland) and filled the interiors with his collection of American antiques. Du Pont's early interests centered on the arts of the Pennsylvania Germans: painted furniture, hooked rugs, redware pottery, and tin, pewter, and iron objects. The collection quickly outgrew the house.

WINTERTHUR: THE NEXT PHASE

Henry Algernon du Pont died on December 31, 1926, at the age of 88, having lived a full and productive life. His only son and heir, Henry Francis, inherited the Winterthur property and soon began planning a large addition to the house—one that would essentially triple its size. The long, narrow extension cut into the steep hillside, allowing for the installation of rooms on either side of central hallways, which provided each with natural light and emphasized a deliberate indoor/outdoor connection. Within this shell, du Pont installed paneling and architectural elements he had purchased from the owners of 17th-, 18th-, and early 19th-century homes along the East Coast that were in danger of demolition. He then decorated each of the "period rooms" with appropriate furnishings.

With the first period rooms at Winterthur, du Pont sought to create a home in the tradition of an English manor house. He displayed his collection of American decorative arts and also entertained family and friends in a grand manner during country-house weekends that included golf, swimming, and numerous bridge games. Thus, the period rooms originally bore names such as Reception Room, Ladies' Room, and Smoking Room. Du Pont completed the first phase of installations in 1931. By 1934 he had begun work on the unaltered section of the house, and between 1935 and 1937 he reinstalled the rooms in the north end with early American architectural interiors. The 1930s house also contained separate suites for the housekeeper, butler, and valet as well as a servants' living room, dining room, and 26 servants' bedrooms.

The last major phase of interior work occurred in the late 1940s, when du Pont was preparing to open his home as a museum. It was then that he supervised the removal of all private family spaces—including bathrooms, dressing rooms, kitchens, and pantries—and replaced them with

The Webb dresser, now part of the
Winterthur collection

Chestertown House, H. F. du Pont's
summer residence in Southampton

Renovation of the north side of the house, ca. 1930

Country-house weekends included bridge
games on the terrace, 1935

View of the house from the south, 1930s

Marian Coffin's East Terrace design

Weekend guests enjoying the pool, 1935

display areas for his collection. Although du Pont strove for historical accuracy in his installations, he was not wedded to it. Rather than portraying exact renditions of past lifestyles, the period rooms are instead extremely influential representations of the Colonial Revival style.

A TALENT FOR GARDENING: SUCCESSION OF BLOOM A love of flowers runs deep in the du Pont family. From Eleuthère Irénée through Henry Francis and continuing to the present, family members have studied and collected botanical specimens and designed great gardens. Two of H. F. du Pont's second cousins in particular—Pierre Samuel and Alfred Irénée—are also remembered for their well-known estates, Longwood Gardens and Nemours.

At Winterthur the landscape provided the perfect setting for a fledgling gardener. The genius of Henry Francis lay in fashioning a garden that looked as though it had always been there, created not by man but by nature. Nothing could have been further from the truth. Over the course of his lifetime, du Pont dug ponds, moved trees, and planted and replanted shrubs and perennials, all to achieve the naturalistic effect. He preferred to guide, rather than force, nature into accomplishing his vision and carefully designed plantings so that there would be a continuous succession of bloom throughout the garden.

In the late 1920s, the addition of the new wing prompted the redesign of the landscaping around the house. To help in this massive undertaking, du Pont turned to his good friend Marian Coffin, a noted landscape architect. Coffin created the landscape plan that integrated the house addition with its surroundings: the Reflecting Pool, East Terrace, and Glade Garden were all part of her masterful design.

THE MUSEUM OPENS In October 1951 Winterthur Museum and grounds opened to the public, and H. F. and Ruth du Pont moved to a new house on the estate that was built for them. The Cottage, as it is known, was constructed in the English Regency style. It overlooks Clenny Run to the south and the garden to the north, providing the perfect spot from which du Pont could continue to oversee daily operations on the property.

After 1951 the estate complex expanded rapidly. In 1959 a new wing to the museum opened; in 1961 a Visitor Center was built to serve the thousands who came to enjoy the garden; in 1969 the Louise du Pont Crowninshield Building, which houses the library and conservation facilities, was dedicated in honor of H. F. du Pont's sister; and in 1992 the Galleries building opened for self-guided tours and the display of changing exhibitions.

Never one to sit idle, H. F. du Pont was as busy as ever. In 1961 he was bestowed with two

The original museum gates, 1951

The Cottage, where H. F. and Ruth du Pont lived after 1951

H. F. du Pont (far left) with Queen Elizabeth and
Prince Philip at the Chelsea Flower Show

honors, recognizing his success with both the Winterthur Garden and his museum collection. The president of the Royal Horticultural Society, who also happened to be an uncle to Queen Elizabeth, asked du Pont to serve as a society vice president. H. F. not only accepted the position but also traveled to the 1962 Chelsea Flower Show, where he was awarded a silver medal for the Winterthur peonies on display.

It was also in 1961 that First Lady Jacqueline Kennedy, who had visited Winterthur, asked H. F. du Pont to chair her Fine Arts Committee for the White House. In turning to the nation's premier authority on American antiques when redecorating her new residence, Mrs. Kennedy was assured of the advice and expertise so necessary for a successful project.

THE DEATHS OF RUTH AND HARRY Ruth Wales du Pont died in 1967. Although the future of his life's work at Winterthur was secure, H. F. remained involved with the running of the estate until the end of his life two years later, on April 11, 1969.

Henry Francis du Pont never enjoyed speaking in public, and he confined his writing to personal correspondence whenever possible. Toward the end of his life, however, he became surprisingly eloquent as he described his vision of Winterthur's future, "I sincerely hope," he noted,

"that the museum will be a continuing source of inspiration and education for all time, and that the gardens and grounds will of themselves be a country place museum where visitors may enjoy as I have, not only the flowers, trees, and shrubs, but also the sunlit meadows, shady wood paths, and the peace and great calm of a country place which has been loved and taken care of for three generations."

H. F. du Pont (standing, right) with Jacqueline Kennedy at the White House

The Period Rooms

In addition to self-guided tours of the collections in the Galleries, visitors to Winterthur may take advantage of numerous guided tours throughout the 175 period rooms in the mansion. We offer here a sampling of the rooms that once housed the du Pont family and their guests.

Port Royal Entrance Hall

Guests arriving at Winterthur after 1931 entered the house through doors brought from Port Royal, a Philadelphia country house built in 1762. As coats were taken by the butler, H. F. du Pont's weekend visitors could look down the hall and view the garden. The interior architecture epitomizes 18th-century design. The classical molding and the Palladian windows represented for du Pont the highest achievement of American craftsmanship. In keeping with the elegance of the architecture, he filled the space with equally tasteful furnishings. The floral design of the 18th-century hand-painted Chinese wallpaper and pattern of the Chinese export porcelain cachepots echo the nearby garden views.

In 1928 H. F. du Pont acquired woodwork and other interior architectural elements from Port Royal, in Philadelphia.

Port Royal Parlor

First-time visitors to Winterthur are always stunned by the beauty of Port Royal Parlor. Arranged with careful attention to symmetry and balance, the room is divided into mirroring halves. Two superb Philadelphia high chests set the stage. Flanking the fireplace are a pair of matching Chippendale sofas that belonged to patriot John Dickinson. Balancing the high chests and sofas are tea tables, side chairs, and easy chairs. A tall desk-and-bookcase stands opposite the fireplace, and the entire arrangement is anchored by a large oriental carpet.

Originally called the Reception Room, Port Royal Parlor was the gathering place for weekend guests upon their arrival. The du Ponts also received their large, extended family here on New Year's Day.

Du Pont Dining Room

The highlight of any weekend visit to Winterthur was the dinner presentation. The table was always set with bouquets, color-coordinated linens (chosen especially to match the seasonal flowers), and elaborate dinnerware, glassware, and silverware. In selecting furnishings for the room, du Pont chose great icons of American decorative arts: the only known set of six silver tankards made by Paul Revere; an unfinished painting by Benjamin West called *American Commissioners;* and a portrait of George Washington by Gilbert Stuart. The furniture is in the Neoclassical, or Federal, style—a taste embraced by the new nation after the American Revolution. Large Chinese export porcelain urns and ceramics recall the young country's entry into the China Trade following the Revolution as do the two knife urns originally owned by Elias Hasket Derby, a Salem entrepreneur who made his fortune in trade with the Far East in the late 1700s.

For the wedding of his daughter Pauline in 1938, H. F. du Pont staged the reception throughout the house but prepared the dining room especially for the bridal party. In a letter to a friend, he described the table decorations: "There we had pink galanthus, orchids in Norwegian silver beakers, and silver candlesticks."

Chinese Parlor

In 1929 du Pont combined three spaces from the original 1839 Bidermann house and created the Chinese Parlor, which serves as a showcase for some extraordinary 18th-century Chinese wallpaper depicting scenes of village life. To accommodate the full length of the rare paper, du Pont had the wall height altered. Rather than cut the paper to fit over the doorways, he commissioned an artist to paint in scenes. The motifs unite the room, which contains 30 pieces of furniture from different regions of colonial America, including Philadelphia, New York, Boston, and Newport. The Chinese theme is further carried out with examples of export porcelain.

Joe Kindig Jr., an antiques dealer and good friend of H. F. du Pont, once remarked, "Harry du Pont is like a conductor of music. He may not know how to play each and every instrument, but he knows how to blend them together, exquisitely."

Montmorenci Stair Hall

In 1935 du Pont replaced his father's imposing entryway and large marble staircase with delicate Neoclassical plaster ornamentation and woodwork from an 1822 plantation home in North Carolina named "Montmorenci." Du Pont purchased the house at auction and adapted its circular staircase to the stair hall at Winterthur. In keeping with the date of the original architecture, he furnished the room with accessories in the classical revival styles, including a matching suite of furniture attributed to the Seymour cabinetmaking family of Boston; a pier table from New York, labeled by Charles-Honoré Lannuier; and a portrait of a young woman in classical dress. The room remains a tribute to du Pont's genius for creating harmonious settings.

In 1935, when the staircase was installed, du Pont took his family on a world tour. Upon returning, daughter Ruth recalled, "It was just fantastic to see that spiral staircase...my father was so pleased that he'd been able to keep it a surprise from my mother and my sister and me...it was dramatic and lovely and beautiful."

Marlboro Room

In creating and furnishing rooms in his "American house," Henry Francis du Pont paid careful attention to selecting objects that gave each space a lived-in look. Nowhere was he more successful than in the Marlboro Room, where he liked to read the paper and where the family gathered each afternoon for tea when they were in residence. The woodwork is from Patuxent Manor, a 1745 house in Lower Marlboro, Maryland. The room contains needlework pictures, portraits by Charles Willson Peale, du Pont family portraits, and Philadelphia furniture. The overall effect is one of simple elegance.

H. F. du Pont prized rarity in the objects he collected. The fishing-lady needlework seen here was created by Sarah Warren in 1748.

Blackwell Parlor

Blackwell Parlor contains the most elaborate setting of any Winterthur period room. The architecture had been part of a 1764 town house built in Philadelphia. Named the Stamper-Blackwell House after its first two owners, it contained intricately carved woodwork. A garland of roses, foliage, and C-scrolls frames the overmantel of the chimney. The undermantel carving illustrates scenes from the fables of La Fontaine. The architecture is the perfect backdrop for the equally ornate and intricately carved Chippendale furniture made in Philadelphia at the same time—both expressive of the mid-century Rococo style in Europe.

A visitor to the Blackwell Parlor gains a sense of the opulent lifestyle of wealthy 18th-century Philadelphians as well as the essential vision of Henry Francis du Pont, who wished to honor the aesthetic vision of colonial Americans.

Fraktur Room

Henry Francis du Pont began his collecting with a focus on the arts of the Pennsylvania Germans. He especially favored their highly decorated sgraffito and slipware pottery, painted furniture, and colorful fraktur. In 1950 du Pont purchased architectural elements from the David Hottenstein house, which was built in Kutztown, Pennsylvania, in 1783. The colorful decorative painting on the wood-work is echoed in the nearby blanket chest as well as in the sgraffito wares. As a counterpoint, du Pont chose the simple elegance of a collection of pewter by William Will, one of Pennsylvania's most noted peweters.

The term *fraktur* comes from the German word meaning "to write fancily." Fraktur commemorate important events such as births, baptisms, and marriages.

Spatterware Hall

One of H. F. du Pont's early collecting passions was spatterware, a type of sponged and painted ceramic with bright, cheerful colors favored by the Pennsylvania German community. Du Pont assembled a comprehensive collection, which was originally displayed at Chestertown House in Southampton. Windsor chairs and hooked rugs from that house are also shown here. These objects reflect the Colonial Revival style, an approach to decorating very much in vogue in the early 1900s.

Ever the gardener, H. F. du Pont's technique of displaying ceramics in masses mirrors his arrangement of flowers in the Winterthur Garden.

Cecil Bedroom

For his own bedroom suite—called Cecil after architecture from
an early 1700s home in Cecil County, Maryland—du Pont chose
a space that overlooks the garden. This softly colored, full-paneled
room was one of the first to be fitted with historic interior woodwork.
Du Pont furnished the rooms with objects in the Queen Anne style,
one of his favorite design periods.

H.F. du Pont's office
formed part of his
bedroom suite. Every
morning, his secretary
and estate foremen
would line up in the
hallway to await
instructions for the day.

Shaker Rooms

At the age of 82, H. F. du Pont oversaw the installation of a set of Shaker Rooms from Enfield, New Hampshire. The Shakers were part of a utopian religious movement that flourished in the United States in the late 18th and early 19th centuries. Dedicating their "hands to work and hearts to God," they lived celibate lives in communities where all property was held in common. "Austere simplicity" perhaps best describes the Shakers' approach to their lives, architecture, and furnishings.

Although the Shakers lived apart, they interacted with the world when it suited them. Members possessed a variety of skills, and Shaker products were esteemed by outsiders for their high standards.

The Court

In the late 1940s, the transformation of the Winterthur house into a museum began in earnest. One of the most laborious undertakings involved creating an indoor courtyard. The Court is surrounded by building exteriors from North Carolina, Rhode Island, Massachusetts, and Delaware: the facade of Montmorenci, from North Carolina; the exterior of a 1756 summerhouse from Middletown, Rhode Island; a doorway from Springfield, Massachusetts; and the 1800s brickfront Red Lion Inn, from Red Lion, Delaware.

The Court was created in the space formerly occupied by the family's badminton court.

The Garden

The garden at Winterthur never fails to delight. Each season presents its own gems.

March Bank

In 1902 du Pont began developing a "wild" garden on a southfacing slope at the front of the house. In an area soon to be known as the March Bank, he put into practice the color theory and succession-of-bloom principles learned from reading the works of several important British gardeners, especially William Robinson and Gertrude Jekyll. Du Pont ordered and planted bulbs in astonishing quantities: 29,000 in 1909 and 39,000 in 1910.

Today the March Bank is a symphony of color that begins in January with the appearance of snowdrops, followed by golden adonis, bright yellow aconites, green-tipped white snowflakes, and pale lavender crocus. It reaches a crescendo in mid-March, when

From 1902 to 1959 H. F. du Pont kept detailed garden notebooks on the succession of bloom.

electric-blue scilla and glory-of-the-snow blanket the ground. Yellow daffodils accent the carpet of blue, which continues into April with Virginia bluebells and masses of white daffodils. In June and July the bank is bright with the blue, white, and orange of hostas, bellflowers, fairy candles, and daylilies.

The March Bank anticipates the year at Winterthur in its compressed sequence of bloom. It was here that du Pont first realized everything a garden could be. He had moved beyond the formal border plantings of his father's generation and began to see the whole Winterthur landscape as his garden.

Peony Garden

Nineteenth-century garden structures anchor either end of the path
that winds through the Peony Garden, which features a long-bloom-
ing collection of herbaceous and tree peonies, most of which were
developed by Dr. A. P. Saunders. From late May well into June, a
dazzling array of bloom lights up the area in a color range of white,
pink, red, yellow, bronze, peach, maroon, and an almost black variety.

Small, white "beehives"
from the Latimeria
estate in Wilmington
live gracefully among
the peonies.

Azalea Woods

Azalea Woods, the best-known garden area on the estate, had a serendipitous beginning. In 1904 a blight wiped out the large stand of chestnut trees in Winterthur's woodland. Several years later, on a visit to one of his favorite nurseries on Long Island, Henry Francis du Pont saw a new azalea—a Kurume hybrid named for the Japanese city where it had been developed. Du Pont purchased 17 of the plants, marking the beginning of Azalea Woods and his many years of experimentation with color and plant combinations.

In Azalea Woods, an understory of white flowering dogwood adds to the blaze of color provided by hundreds of white, pink, salmon, and red azaleas in early May. This breathtaking display is closely followed by the flowering of Dexter hybrid rhododendrons. And thousands of Spanish bluebells and wildflowers carpet the forest floor throughout April and May.

Azalea Woods covers eight acres of the estate.

Magnolia Bend

At the end of the March Bank, the pathway bends and broadens into Garden Lane. Tucked into this bend is a stand of saucer magnolias, one of the true glories of the early spring garden. Nearby, magnificent Sargent cherry trees stand like sentinels. In recent garden restorations, new plantings in tones of white, blue, and lavender have extended the bloom period throughout the summer and into fall: summer snowflake viburnum, white rugosa roses, lavender Russian sage, and blue plumbago.

The oldest saucer magnolias in this area were planted by Henry Algernon du Pont around 1880.

Winterhazel Walk

Nowhere is the color genius of Henry Francis du Pont more apparent than in Winterhazel Walk. Several species of winterhazel grace the garden area, their soft greenish-yellow blossoms contrasting with the intermingled plantings of lavender-flowering Korean rhododendrons. These dual blooms appear before most of the deciduous spring leaves have unfurled, increasing their impact. Flowing beneath the shrubs are waves of harmonious color provided by hellebores, corydalis, and primroses.

Winterhazel Walk illustrates one of the canons of garden design to which du Pont firmly adhered: once the major plants have been selected for a garden area, add others that bloom simultaneously to complete the composition as well as those that bloom earlier and later than the main event, to give the area a gradual beginning and end.

In 1920 H. F. du Pont began his color experimentation with winterhazel and rhododendrons.

Pinetum

In 1918, when Charles Sprague Sargent, the first director of Arnold Arboretum in Massachusetts, learned that his friend Henry Algernon du Pont was interested in establishing a Pinetum, he enthusiastically wrote, "I am very much interested in a Pinetum in Delaware...one is needed in your region."

In the winter landscape, the Pinetum stands out as an oasis of green. As the earliest shrubs and small trees come into flower, the dense evergreens provide a dark accent for the spring blossoms.

In the 1930s and 1940s, Henry Francis enlivened his father's evergreen plantings by adding flowering shrubs to form paths throughout the area.

Sundial Garden

In 1955 Henry Francis du Pont and landscape architect Marian Coffin joined forces to create the Sundial Garden. Situated on the former site of the estate tennis courts, the space presented one of the few level planting areas in the garden. Using the Pinetum and an evergreen hedge as the walls, Coffin filled the enclosure with lush, fragrant shrubs: magnolias, cherries, quince, crab apples, viburnum, spirea, fothergillas, lilacs, pearlbushes, and roses—arranged in concentric circles around an antique armillary sundial.

This magnificent "garden room" is the highlight of the landscape in April.

Sycamore Hill

Located near the boundary separating the garden area from the agricultural landscape, a magnificent 200-year-old sycamore tree holds sway, surrounded by trees, shrubs, and plants that flower in succession from April through October. In late May and early June, the white blooms of mock orange, deutzias, and kousa dogwoods predominate in color, accompanied by accent notes of lilacs, fountain buddleias, red weigela, and mountain laurel.

This area of the landscape shaded grazing dairy cows when Winterthur was a working farm.

Quarry Garden

In 1962, at the age of 82, Henry Francis du Pont and his crew of gardeners created the Quarry Garden, fashioned from an abandoned site that had once supplied the stone used in constructing Winterthur's walls and bridges. The gardeners positioned huge rock slabs to extend the natural outcroppings and created crevices to fill with a rich assortment of perennials and shrubs. This garden area reaches its peak in early June, when masses of candelabra primroses fill the boggy floor with color.

H. F. du Pont was never afraid to mix colors, as seen with these primroses.

Enchanted Woods

Years ago, generations of young du Ponts enjoyed playing in an area that today is home to Enchanted Woods™, the children's garden at Winterthur. Created in 2001, the space is designed as a unified garden rather than a playground, featuring the Acorn Tea Room, Serpentine Path, Tulip Tree House, Faerie Cottage, Bird's Nest, Frog Hollow, and Forbidden Fairy Ring. Numerous plantings add color, texture, and fragrance. "Fairy cups," the drooping bells of cowslip, and the sweetly scented bells of lily of the valley—a favorite flower of Henry Francis du Pont—can be found throughout the woods.

This delightful area of the garden is filled with child-size features.

Reflecting Pool

The Reflecting Pool garden area was one of Marian Coffin's major projects at Winterthur. In developing a landscaping plan that would mask the size of the 1928–31 addition to the Winterthur house, Coffin turned to the great gardens of the Italian Renaissance for inspiration. Relying on the principles of axial symmetry and proportion, she designed a grand staircase leading from the East Terrace to the family swimming pool, which is now called the Reflecting Pool. Flanked by twin bathhouses and surrounded by a low stone wall, the area is the perfect setting for contemplation.

Water lilies fill the Reflecting Pool during the summer months.

Glade Garden

Near the Reflecting Pool is the Glade Garden, a shady summer refuge with naturalistic pools and waterfalls created from 100 tons of imported limestone. The ponds are home to frogs, koi, and small turtles, making it a favorite stopping place for families.

Daylilies, lacecap hydrangeas, bellflowers, and hostas bloom abundantly in early summer.

Greenhouses have been part of the Winterthur landscape since 1839. This complex, begun in 1903-4, once included a winter vegetable garden, a fig house, a dahlia house, a rose house with special pink roses, and space for palms, chrysanthemums, orchids and annuals.

Greenhouses
68

Walking Tour of the Estate

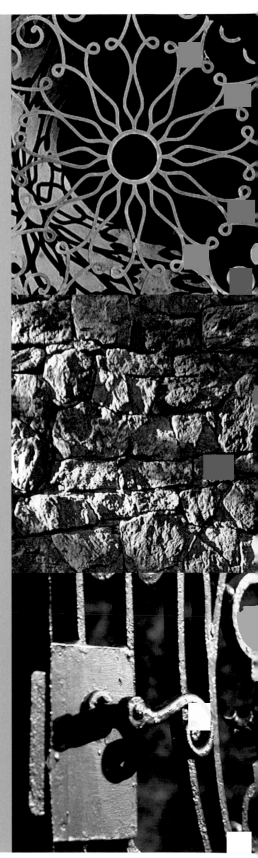

As you stroll along the walkways and garden paths of the estate, learn more about our unique history. Look for the dark-blue Heritage Markers that appear on various buildings.

Visitor Center

Built in 1961, Winterthur's Visitor Center exists in harmony with the nearby woodlands. Its low roof and glass walls allow unobstructed views of the surrounding landscape. Initially constructed as a lunch pavilion for visitors on the Spring Tour, its role has expanded over the years. The building now features a restaurant, lecture hall, and bookstore and functions as the site for special events, including weddings.

Butler's House

Colonel Henry Algernon du Pont purchased this house and 100
acres of surrounding woodland from the Joseph Chandler family in
1900. He then altered the exterior by applying stucco over the brick
and adding two enclosed porches. The building is typical of workers'
housing on the Winterthur estate. Generations of du Pont butlers
and their families lived in this house, hence its name. Today the
building contains staff offices.

Fire Station

Although farmworkers always served as members of the fire bri-
gade throughout the estate's history, the official Winterthur Fire
Department was not founded until 1957. This structure, built in 1960
on the site of an old frame house, contains state-of-the-art firefight-
ing equipment. Members of Winterthur staff still serve as firefighters
and receive extensive and ongoing training.

Greenhouses

Greenhouses have been a part of the Winterthur landscape since 1839. The complex seen here was begun in 1903–4, when two of the greenhouses built by the Bidermanns were moved to the site and three new ones were added, complete with ventilation, heating, and water. Over the years the structures have included a winter vegetable garden, a fig house, a dahlia house, a rose house, and space for palms, orchids, chrysanthemums, and annuals. Flowers played an important part in the lives of each generation of du Ponts on the estate. H. F. du Pont in particular took immense pride in the profusion of blooms that filled every corner of the house.

Potting Sheds & Cold Frames

Between 1930 and 1969, cold frames (used to protect seedlings)
covered more than one acre of ground at Winterthur. An enormous
cement potting shed provided the running water and storage space
needed by the large gardening staff. These areas are still used by the
Winterthur Garden Department.

1750 House

Hidden within this building is the museum's main air-conditioning system. The exterior of the house combines Winterthur's 19th-century water tower with the gable end of an 18th-century Delaware house built by Colonel Alexander E. Porter for his farm south of New Castle. That structure was slated for demolition in 1963 when H. F. du Pont bought it and had it moved to Winterthur. Speakers were once mounted on the roof of the 1750 House so du Pont could listen to music while on his golf course, which was just on the far side of Azalea Woods.

Coach House

This building, located on the banks of nearby Clenny Run, housed horses and coaches in the early 20th century. Later it stored Henry Francis du Pont's fleet of cars. The upper section of the Coach House served as a boardinghouse for the chauffeurs and servants of guests who came for Winterthur's fabled country-house weekends. Today that area contains staff offices, and the lower level houses the Winterthur Post Office.

The Cottage

Henry Francis and Ruth du Pont moved to this house in 1951, after their family home opened to the public as a museum. The Cottage, constructed in the English Regency style, stands on the site of the original estate farmhouse. Today the Cottage contains the Museum Store and Plant Shop as well as staff offices.

Conservatory

Before 1929, a porte cochere protected Winterthur guests and family from foul weather as they arrived at the house. In 1930 that structure was removed and replaced by this expansive conservatory. When the family was in residence, lavish floral displays filled the space.

East Terrace

When Henry Francis du Pont expanded the house in the late 1920s and early 1930s, he preserved as many of the tulip-poplars and American beeches as possible. Working with landscape architect Marian Coffin, he created a garden area with stone balustrades and an elegant summerhouse. Today the East Terrace provides a transition between the museum and the surrounding naturalistic garden.

Bathhouses

Built in 1929, Winterthur's twin bathhouses provided space for family members and weekend guests who enjoyed the swimming pool. A stereo system is hidden behind the circular grillwork in the stone wall that connects the two houses. Du Pont particularly liked opera, and his guests were often treated to recordings of arias while they sunned and swam.

Louise du Pont Crowninshield Building

Constructed in 1969 on the site of the former rose garden, the
Crowninshield wing was named in honor of Louise, Henry Francis
du Pont's sister and a founder of the National Trust for Historic
Preservation. Today it houses the library, conservation facilities, and
research laboratory and connects to the Dorrance Gallery, which
features the Campbell Collection of Soup Tureens.

The Galleries

Opened in 1992, the two-story Galleries building provides space
for the display of selections from the permanent collection as well as
special traveling exhibitions. Self-guided tours allow for a leisurely
viewing of an orientation video in addition to furniture, ceramics,
glass, textiles, metalwork, paintings, and prints from the Winterthur
collection.

Train Station

Since 1867 railroad tracks have run through the Winterthur estate. The Wilmington and Northern Railroad (of which Henry Algernon du Pont was president) used the line primarily to transport freight. For many years the Train Station housed the Winterthur Post Office as well as living quarters for the postmistress. Today the building provides meeting space for Winterthur staff and for special events.

The Graduate Programs

Shortly after the museum opened to the public, a new chapter in Winterthur's history began. H. F. du Pont realized that the research and care of decorative arts collections such as his would require the advice and expertise of specialists. Therefore, in conjunction with the University of Delaware, the Winterthur Program in Early American Culture (WPEAC) was established in 1952 to educate aspiring curators in the material culture of decorative arts objects. Since that time more than 400 students have graduated from the two-year program and can be found working at major museums and historic houses in the United States. So marked was the success of the program that in 1974, five years after du Pont's death, a second graduate program was founded with the University of Delaware. The Winterthur-University of Delaware Program in Art Conservation (WUDPAC) offers a three-year course of study in the conservation of historic objects, providing specialized training for much-needed professionals. Its 200+ graduates are recognized throughout the world for their commitment to the preservation of cultural heritage.

Copyright © 2005 The Henry Francis du Pont Winterthur
Museum, Inc.

Compiled by Pauline K. Eversmann with research
assistance by Maggie Lidz

All Rights Reserved. No part of this publication may be
reproduced or transmitted in any form or by any means,
electronic or mechanical, including photocopying,
recording, or any information retrieval system, without
written permission of Winterthur Publications, Winterthur,
Delaware, 19735.

Distributed by University Press of New England

DESIGN: Studio Blue, Chicago, www.studioblueinc.com
EDITOR: Onie Rollins
ESTATE MAP DESIGN: Tom Willcockson, Mapcraft.com

LIBRARY OF CONGRESS CATALOGING-IN-PUBLICATION DATA
Eversmann, Pauline K., 1942–
Guide to Winterthur Museum & Country Estate / compiled
by Pauline K. Eversmann ; with research assistance by
Maggie Lidz.—1st ed.
    p. cm.
 ISBN-13: 978-0-912724-65-2 (alk. paper)
1. Henry Francis du Pont Winterthur Museum—
Guidebooks. 2. Decorative arts—United States. 3.
Decorative arts—Delaware—Winterthur—Guidebooks.
4. Henry Francis du Pont Winterthur Museum Gardens
(Del.)—Guidebooks. I. Lidz, Maggie, 1958–
II. Title.
 NK460.W48H4535 2005
 745'.074'7511—dc22
                                              2005017788

PHOTO CREDITS
Gavin Ashworth 26–27, 30–31, 35, 38–39, 40–41, 42–43; Linda
Eirhart 67; Michael Gunselman 4, 24, 57, 58, 62 (right),
76–77, 78, 82–83, 85, 86–91, 92 (right & bottom), 93–95, 96
(left), 97–99, 100 (left), 101; Hagley Museum 9; Gottlieb
Hampfler 81; Lizzie Himmel 28; Ruth Joyce 54, 56, 59, 60, 62
(right), 63, 64–65, 66, 68, 70, 72–73, 74–75, 79 (right), 80, 84;
Russ Kennedy 82 (left); Robert Lautman 69; Ray Magnani
55; Schoonover Studios 10 (top); Stromberg/Gunther 102.
All others, courtesy Winterthur.

Winterthur Museum & Country Estate